God's
REMEDY for
REJECTION

God's
REMEDY for
REJECTION

DEREK PRINCE

Whitaker House

GOD'S REMEDY FOR REJECTION

Derek Prince
Derek Prince Ministries-International
P.O. Box 19501
Charlotte, NC 28219

ISBN: 0-88368-483-7
Printed in the United States of America
Copyright © 1993 by Derek Prince Ministries-International
Images © 1995 PhotoDisc, Inc.

Whitaker House
30 Hunt Valley Circle
New Kensington, PA 15068

Contents

1

The Nature
of
Rejection

The Nature of Rejection

Almost all of us have experienced rejection at one time or another, but many of us have not understood its nature or its effects. The rejection may have been something relatively minor—or it may have been so devastating that it affected your whole life and all your relationships.

Here are some common examples: you were not chosen to play on a school sports team; your first boyfriend failed to show up for an important date and never gave you a reason; you were not accepted at the college of your choice; you were laid off from your job for no good reason—they said you were "redundant."

Far worse than these examples is the pain that comes because you never felt love from your father, because you sensed your mother didn't want you, or because your marriage ended in divorce.

Experiences such as these leave permanent wounds, whether you are aware of them or not. But I have good news for you! God can heal you from the wounds that come from rejection, help you to accept yourself, and enable you to show His love to others. However, before you can receive His help, you must recognize the nature of your problem.

Rejection can be defined as the sense of being unwanted. You desire people to love you, and yet you believe that they do not. You want to be part of a group, but you feel excluded. Somehow you are always on the outside looking in.

Closely related to rejection are the wounds of betrayal and shame. All produce similar responses in the wounded person, the feeling of not being wanted or accepted.

The Nature of Rejection

Sometimes rejection is so wounding and painful that the mind refuses to focus on it. Nevertheless, you know something is there—even though it is deeper than the mind, deeper than the reason, deeper than the memory. It is in your spirit. The book of Proverbs describes this:

> *13 A happy heart makes the face cheerful, but heartache crushes the spirit.*
> (Proverbs 15:13)

The writer also tells how a crushed spirit will affect a person:

> *14 A man's spirit sustains him in sickness, but a crushed spirit who can bear?* (Proverbs 18:14)

A vibrant spirit helps a person through great difficulties, but a crushed spirit has a crippling effect in all areas of life.

Our society today is suffering from a progressive breakdown of interpersonal relationships. Quite possibly you have been caught in the crossfire, and the result has been a wound of rejection. Let me suggest, however, that you should look for a silver lining to that dark cloud.

I believe the Devil has some foreknowledge. He knows God wants to use you, and he has struck his blow first. In a way it is a kind of twisted compliment. It means that Satan is afraid of what you can become in Christ. So, do not be discouraged. In my experience I have found that the people who have been the lowest often end up the highest. The Scriptures tell us, *"He who humbles himself will be exalted"* (Luke 18:14).

There is a verse in Matthew that I believe describes how Jesus feels toward you:

> [36] *But when He saw the multitudes, He was moved with compassion for them...* (Matthew 9:36a NKJV)

The Greek word translated "compassion" is amazingly powerful. It implies a forceful, physical reaction in a person's body in the abdominal area. It is a reaction so strong that it demands a response. A person who is *"moved with compassion"* cannot stand by and observe. He must do something. Why was Jesus so moved?

> [36] *...because they were weary and scattered, like sheep having no shepherd.* (Matthew 9:36b NKJV)

12

That is just how you may feel: weary, harried, frustrated, perplexed, fearful, anxious, burdened down. Jesus sees you, just as He saw the multitudes. He has compassion for you. He is longing to heal you where you hurt the most.

First, we must understand the true nature of rejection. How does rejection occur? What causes the wounding? When we answer these questions, then we can ask, How can wounds of rejection be treated?

About 1964 I often found myself ministering to people who were bound by addictions to substances such as nicotine or alcohol. Very quickly, however, I discovered that addictions such as these are merely twigs that have sprouted from a branch. Normally, the branch that supports them is some form of frustration. Therefore, the practical solution is to deal with the branch. When the branch of frustration is cut off, dealing with the twigs of addiction is relatively easy.

As I continued to wrestle with people's personal problems, I gradually worked my way down the trunk of the tree until I came to the part of the tree that lies below the surface—that is, the roots. It is here that God seeks to work in our lives.

> [10] *And even now the ax is laid to the root of the trees. Therefore every tree which does not bear good fruit is cut down and thrown into the fire.*
>
> (Matthew 3:10 NKJV)

From where is the tree cut down? From the roots. When I got down below the surface, I made a discovery that surprised me at first. One of the most common roots of all personal problems is rejection. I reached this conclusion, not as a sociologist or as a psychologist, but as a preacher and a Bible teacher.

Have you ever seen a small child in his father's arms? One little hand clutches the lapel of his father's jacket while his head is pressed against that strong, protective chest. Pressures and tensions may be all around, but the child is not threatened. His face registers total security. He is where he belongs—in his Daddy's arms.

God designed human nature so that every baby born into the world would crave this kind of security. A child can never truly be satisfied, fulfilled, or secure without parental love, particularly love from a father.

Any person who has been deprived of this kind of love is inevitably exposed to the wound of rejection. Almost an entire generation of American fathers have failed their children. Thus, we have a generation of young people whose deepest, most basic problem is rejection.

To this picture of broken relationships between parents and children, we must add the statistics for failed marriages. Today, that covers about half of all marriages. Almost always, one or both parties emerge with a wound of rejection. Very often, there is the added pain of betrayed trust.

When we consider the pressures of today's society, particularly the breakup of family life, my conviction is that at least half of the people in the United States suffer from some form of rejection. No doubt God foresaw this special end-time crisis of broken relationships when He gave this promise in Malachi:

⁵ See, I will send you the prophet Elijah before that great and dreadful day

of the LORD comes.
⁶ He will turn the hearts of the fathers
to their children, and the hearts of the
children to their fathers; or else I will
come and strike the land with a curse.

(Malachi 4:5–6)

The final outcome of rejection caused by broken relationships is a curse. However, for those who will turn to God through Jesus, He has provided healing from this curse.

What form will this healing take? What is the opposite of rejection? Acceptance, of course. This is precisely what God offers you when you come to Him through Jesus. *"He has made us accepted in the Beloved"* (Ephesians 1:6 NKJV)—that is, in Jesus.

(favored one) *Christ*

The original Greek word that is translated here as "accepted" is very powerful. It is much stronger than mere approval. In the New King James Version of Luke 1:28, the same Greek word is translated *"highly favored one."*

favored one

When you come to God through Jesus, you are as accepted and as highly favored as Jesus Himself is. Amazing as it may seem, God loves you in just the same way

He loves Jesus. You become a member of His own family.

The first step in overcoming rejection is to recognize the problem. Once you recognize it, you can deal with it. You are not alone in this; God will help you recognize it.

Let me give you a practical illustration. During World War II, when I was a medical orderly in the desert in North Africa, I was working with a man who was a brilliant doctor. A bomb fell from an enemy plane and exploded somewhere near us. One of our soldiers was struck with a piece of shrapnel. He came into the medical station with this tiny, black puncture mark in his shoulder. As a result, I was very busy attending to him, cleaning his wound, and trying to do the right thing, when I asked the doctor, "Shall I get out a dressing?"

The doctor said, "No, give me the probe." So, I handed him the little silver stick, and he put it in the wound and moved it around. Nothing happened for a few moments. Suddenly, the probe touched the little piece of shrapnel inside, and the patient let out a yelp. The doctor knew he had found the problem.

When I again asked if I should bring the dressing, the doctor replied, "No, bring me the forceps." He put the forceps in and removed the piece of shrapnel. Only then did he want to apply the dressing.

You may be putting a little dressing of religion over a wound that cannot heal because there is something inside that is causing it to fester. However, if you will open your heart to the Holy Spirit, He will reveal the source of the problem. If the Holy Spirit's probe touches a piece of shrapnel, yelp if you must, but don't resist! Ask Him to use His forceps to remove the problem. Then God can apply something that will really heal it.

As you read on, you will discover how you can move from rejection to acceptance. Along the way, you will also learn how to deal with betrayal and shame. After that, I will show you how to let God's divine love flow through you to other people.

I have dealt with many, many people who have successfully recognized and recovered from the wounds of rejection. You can be one of those people through God's grace.

2

The Causes
of
Rejection

The Causes of
Rejection

All human relationships are accompanied by the risk of rejection. Sometimes rejection comes during the school years. Perhaps you wore hand-me-down clothes, or you were of a different race, or you had a physical defect, so you were singled out for ridicule at your school. Many people are disturbed by those who are different. If they do not know how to identify with you, they reject you.

The most damaging kind of rejection comes when a child perceives rejection from a parent. There are, perhaps, three main situations that can cause this wound. First, a child may be unwanted during pregnancy. The mother may be carrying a child in her womb whom she really does not want. She may not say anything, but the attitude is in her heart. The child may have been conceived outside of marriage. She may come to resent and hate this thing that is coming into her life that will create all kinds of problems for her. Such a child may be born with a spirit of rejection.

I discovered an amazing phenomenon in ministering to people in the United States. Very commonly, people in a certain age group seemed to have this sense of early rejection. When I traced it back, I discovered they had been born during the Great Depression. I came to understand that a mother at that time, with many mouths to feed, could hardly bear the thought of having to struggle with one more child. Her inner attitude wounded that child before it ever came forth from her womb.

A second situation is when a child's parents do not physically demonstrate their love for their child. Bumper stickers used to ask, "Have you hugged your child today?" That is a good question. A child who receives little physical affection or touch tends to become a rejected child.

Even if parents love their child, they may not know how to express their love. I have talked to people recently who say, "I suppose my father loved me, but he never knew how to show it. All his life he never sat me on his knee; he never did anything to show me that he loved me." It may be that the child feels rejection from the mother, instead, but in either case the child thinks, "I'm unwanted."

If you talk to many children today who are bitter and rebellious toward their parents, they will tell you this: "Our parents gave us clothes and an education and a car and a swimming pool, but they never gave us time. They never gave us themselves."

This, I think, is one reason for the bitter reaction we saw in the 1960s of young people against the older generations. It was a reaction against loveless materialism. Many of those young people who became so bitter and rebellious were from rather privileged, wealthy homes. They had been given everything except love, which was the thing they wanted and needed most.

This form of rejection may also affect a child whose parents have divorced. Usually it is the mother who is left to care for the children by herself. The child of such a divorce may have had a warm, loving relationship with the father, but suddenly the father is no longer there. His leaving creates an aching void in the child's heart.

If the father has gone off with another woman, the child's reaction is twofold: bitterness toward the father and hatred toward the other woman. What the child now has is a deep wound of rejection, something that says, "The person I loved and trusted the most has abandoned me. From now on I can never trust anyone."

Often, too, the mother, with many new responsibilities thrust upon her, may not be able to give the child the affection she formerly lavished upon him or her. In this case the child experiences a double rejection: from the father and from the mother.

A third rejection-producing circumstance occurs when siblings perceive unequal affection from their parents, whether it is intentional or not. I have noticed that a family with three children may have a first child who is clever and knows all the answers. As the first child, he enjoys a natural priority. The next child comes along and is not so brilliant. Then the third child is cute and bright. The second child continually feels inferior to the others. Somehow, the parents are always praising the oldest child or the youngest, but they do not say much about the middle child. In many cases that middle child feels rejected and unwanted. He or she thinks, "My parents love my older brother and my younger sister, but they don't love me."

On the other hand, instead of one child in the family experiencing rejection, sometimes one child receives an unfair measure of love and attention at the expense of the siblings. The other children, just by comparing themselves with that particularly favored child, feel rejected.

I remember a story about a mother who had several daughters but favored one above the rest. One day she heard a sound in another room. Thinking it was the daughter she particularly loved, she called out, "Is that you, darling?" The discouraged voice of another daughter was heard in reply, "No, it's only me."

Then the mother realized the impact that her favoritism for the one daughter had left on the others. She repented and sought to repair the damaged relationships with all of her children.

Let me give you another example of how rejection can occur at a very young age and of the spiritual impact it can have on a child. Many years ago I was conducting services at a church in Miami. While visiting one of the parishioners at home a few nights earlier, I had done something I rarely do. I said to her, "Sister, if I'm correct, you have the spirit of death in you."

She had every reason to be happy, but she never was. She had a good husband and children, yet she hardly ever smiled or looked happy. She was like a person in continual mourning. Although I very rarely make that kind of statement to anybody, I felt I had to say something to her that night.

I said, "I'm preaching on Friday night in Miami. If you come, I'll pray for you."

At the beginning of the meeting, I noticed her sitting in the front row. Once again, I did something I do not usually do.

At a certain point in the service, I walked over to her and said, "You spirit of death, in the name of Jesus, I command you to answer me now. When did you enter this woman?"

And the spirit, not the woman, answered very clearly, "When she was two years old."

I said, "How did you get in?"

Again it was the spirit that answered, "Oh, she felt rejected; she felt unwanted; she felt lonely."

Later that evening, the woman was delivered from the spirit of death, but for several days that incident kept coming back to my mind. It gave me a new understanding of the effect that rejection can have on a person's life. It is not merely evil in itself, but it also opens the door for various other negative, destructive forces to move in and gradually take over a person's life. Rejection truly is a root from which much that is harmful can grow.

Since that time, I have dealt with several hundred people who needed and received deliverance from the spiritual effects of rejection.

The woman in that example was obviously distressed, but rejection is not always outwardly visible. Rejection can be a hidden, inner attitude that we carry around. The problem lies in the area of the spirit. I have learned by experience that every negative emotion, reaction, and attitude have associated with them a corresponding spirit. Behind fear is a spirit of fear; behind jealousy is a spirit of jealousy; behind hate is a spirit of hate.

This does not mean that every person who experiences fear, for instance, has a spirit of fear. However, a person who fails to exercise self-control and habitually or unrestrainedly gives in to fear will probably open the way for a spirit of fear to enter. After that, the person is no longer in full control of himself or herself.

This also applies to other emotions such as jealousy or hate. In many cases rejection opens the way for the other negative spirits to follow. As already stated, rejection is a root from which many destructive emotions and attitudes may grow.

Here is an example of how the process may work. A young girl feels rejected by her father and hates him because he is critical and unloving. This hatred deepens to a point where she can no longer suppress it.

When she becomes an adult, she marries and has children of her own. In due course, she finds herself hating one of her own children. Her hatred is vicious and unreasonable, but she cannot control it. This is a spirit of hate. When the father is no longer present, the hatred is directed against some other family member.

Another effect of the spirit of hatred may cause her to hate all men. She may even become a lesbian and avoid all healthy contact with men.

In the next chapter, we turn to a form of rejection that far too many people have experienced in deep, close relationships—betrayal of trust. I also describe how shame often accompanies this kind of experience.

3

Betrayal
and
Shame

Betrayal and Shame

Previously, we discussed some of the primary causes of rejection in early childhood. As we grow older, we expose ourselves to the possibility of even more rejection as the bonds of intimate, close relationships form in us. If we are rejected in one of these relationships, especially by a marriage partner, the pain is compounded because it involves broken trust, and thus it becomes betrayal.

Like most other ministers, numerous times I have counseled wives who feel that they have lost everything. They trusted

their husbands and gave themselves unre-
servedly. Then their husbands left them.
The wives felt betrayed. I have also talked
to husbands who have been betrayed by
their wives. I have also seen many other
varieties of betrayal.

Have you been betrayed? How have
you responded?

When someone betrays you, you may
say, "I'll never open myself up again. No
one will ever get another chance to hurt me
like that." That is a natural reaction, but it
is also dangerous. It will open you up to a
second problem, defensiveness, which is
the reaction of somebody who has been
hurt once too often. Defensiveness says,
"All right, I'll go through life, but I will
never let anybody come near enough to
hurt me like that again. I'll always keep a
wall between me and other people."

Do you know who suffers? You do. Your
personality shrivels, becoming incomplete.
You grow as a tree does when its main
trunk is lopped off—in a distorted manner.

In Isaiah we find a vivid picture of what
betrayal is like. The Lord was comforting
His people Israel through Isaiah. God

painted for them a picture of their condition as He saw it. He compared them to a wife who has been rejected by her husband. This same situation is distressingly all too familiar for millions of women today, yet the Lord still offers these same comforting words:

> [4] *"Do not be afraid; you will not suffer shame. Do not fear disgrace; you will not be humiliated. You will forget the shame of your youth and remember no more the reproach of your widowhood.*
> [5] *"For your Maker is your husband— the LORD Almighty is his name—the Holy One of Israel is your Redeemer; he is called the God of all the earth.*
> [6] *"The LORD will call you back as if you were a wife deserted and distressed in spirit—a wife who married young, only to be rejected,"* says your God.   (Isaiah 54:4–6)

The illustration reaches its zenith in the last verse with the image of a *"wife deserted and distressed in spirit—a wife who married young, only to be rejected."* Many of you may know how that feels.

Sometimes it is the other way around; sometimes the wife rejects her husband.

Although we regard men as somehow being stronger than women, I know from the many cases with which I have dealt that a man who feels rejected by his wife can suffer inexpressible agony. He may feel he has failed as a man. In some ways, perhaps, it is harder for a man to experience that kind of hurt because he feels ashamed of it. Our society expects men to be impervious to emotional pain.

This vivid picture in Isaiah highlights two things that are commonly associated with betrayal in marriage. Through Isaiah the Lord says, *"You will not suffer shame... You will not be humiliated."* To have given yourself without reservation to another person, to have poured out your love upon him, to have made yourself available to him, and then to discover that he has rejected you—the sum of all that can bring with it shame and humiliation.

You are suffering from shame if somehow you feel that you are not fit to meet other people or that you cannot look anyone straight in the face. People who are suffering from shame will often avert or lower their eyes when approached by another person. Shame is debilitating, and it keeps us from functioning as healthy human beings.

In addition to betrayal through divorce, two other common ways in which shame affects a person's spirit are through public humiliation and child abuse.

Public humiliation often happens in a school setting. For example, my wife and I were acquainted with a fine, young Jewish man—we will call him Max—who had accepted the Messiah but still had problems. As we were speaking with him one time, I detected a sense of shame. When we asked him about this, his mind went back to high school. At the end of the school year, the headmaster had announced in front of all the other students that Max was the only one who had failed and that he would have to repeat his classes the following year.

From that time on, Max was never exactly the person he ought to have been. He covered it up. He was very active and aggressive in order to prove he was the best. However, if you have to struggle all the time to prove you are as good as others, something is wrong. Max needed to recognize and acknowledge shame at work in his life.

Another way betrayal and shame come in is through sexual or physical abuse in childhood. Both are distressingly common in our society. A child may not be free to tell anyone else about it. Often it is a parent, grandparent, or another relative who is responsible for the abuse. The abused child never knows whether to trust that relative again. Thus, the person continually struggles with mixed attitudes: on the one hand, mistrust; on the other, the obligation to show respect. How can a child honor a parent who has abused him or her?

A person may go through life without ever resolving that tension. It remains a shameful secret. However, you can always open up to the Lord and tell Him all your hidden secrets. You never embarrass or shock Him, and He will never reject you. You can tell Him the worst thing that ever happened to you, and He will respond, "I knew it all along, and I still love you."

Even though God offers us full acceptance, our realization of His love is often blocked by the far-reaching consequences of rejection, betrayal, and shame, which I will describe in the next chapter.

4

The Results
of
Rejection

The Results of Rejection

I believe the primary result of rejection is the inability to receive or communicate love. A person who has never experienced being loved cannot transmit love. Scripture expresses that truth this way:

[19] *We love because* [God] *first loved us.*
                                 (1 John 4:19)

It is the love of God that stimulates our love for Him in response. Love lies dormant until it is stimulated by another person. Without such interaction, love never comes to life.

Hence, if a person does not know the love of God or parents, an inability to love can be passed from generation to generation. For example, a little girl is born into a family where she does not experience love. She has a wound of rejection, so she cannot communicate love. She grows up, marries, becomes a mother, and has a daughter. Because she cannot communicate love to her daughter, her daughter has the same problem. Thus, this terrible problem is perpetuated from generation to generation.

In ministering to such people, I have often said, "At some point this thing must be stopped. Why not let it happen now so that you don't continue passing on rejection to the next generation? Is rejection the legacy you want to leave to your children?"

God spoke through Ezekiel that children should not be obligated to suffer for what their ancestors did wrong:

> [1] *The word of the LORD came to me:*
> [2] *"What do you people mean by quoting this proverb about the land of Israel: 'The fathers eat sour grapes, and*

the children's teeth are set on edge'?
³ *"As surely as I live, declares the Sovereign LORD, you will no longer quote this proverb in Israel.*
⁴ *"For every living soul belongs to me, the father as well as the son—both alike belong to me. The soul who sins is the one who will die....*
⁹ *"He* [who] *follows my decrees and faithfully keeps my laws. That man is righteous; he will surely live, declares the Sovereign LORD."*

(Ezekiel 18:1–4, 9)

Thus, even if your parents never showed you love, God does not want you or your children to suffer for their mistakes. By accepting God's provision, you can cut off that evil inheritance once and for all.

Besides an inability to show love, there are other secondary results of rejection. I would say rejection produces three kinds of people: the person who gives in, the person who holds out, and the person who fights back.

First, let's look at the person who gives in. This type of person thinks, "I just can't take this. Life is too much for me. There is really nothing I can do."

I have learned by experience in dealing with such people that it opens the way for a descending series of negative emotions or attitudes that goes like this:

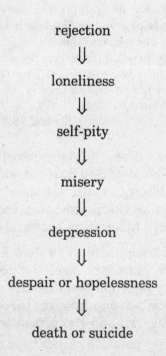

rejection
⇓
loneliness
⇓
self-pity
⇓
misery
⇓
depression
⇓
despair or hopelessness
⇓
death or suicide

The final result is tragic. Many, of course, stop short of it, yet it is the logical outcome of the process that is set in motion by rejection. Whether it takes the form of death or of suicide depends on the emotional makeup of each person. Someone whose reactions are essentially passive will ultimately succumb to death. Rejection is, in fact, a contributing factor in many deaths that are attributed merely to natural causes.

A person who follows the path to death has an inner desire to die. Have you ever made a remark such as, "I'd be better off dead," or "What's the use of living?" That is a very dangerous way to speak. It is an invitation to the spirit of death to enter.

In contrast, a person with a more aggressive attitude will turn to suicide as a radical solution. Such people may also ask themselves, "What's the use of living?" However, they will add, "I might as well end it all."

Often the more aggressive person sees suicide as a way to hurt those who have caused his pain. The inner thought pattern is something like this: "I'll get even with them. Now they'll suffer the way I have!"

The latest figures for suicides among young people in America are frightening.

More than five thousand youths between the ages of five and twenty-four committed suicide in 1990, according to the National Center for Health statistics.

In most cases the undiagnosed root cause of these suicides was rejection. They probably could not express it in words, but deep down these young people felt unwanted and unimportant.

Are you beginning to realize that you have some of the symptoms I have described? If you find you are losing control over your own responses, it may well be that you are not just struggling with your own negative attitudes. A demonic influence may be at work exploiting those attitudes.

Do not close your mind to this possibility. Coming to grips with your problem can be a big step toward overcoming it. In a later chapter, I will show you how to pray against this kind of evil influence.

The second personality pattern produced by rejection is the type of person who refuses to give in and builds some kind of defense. This is really a facade, something that covers up the inner agony and struggle.

Someone who is building up a defense for himself usually develops a kind of superficial happiness. The person appears to be outgoing and is probably talkative, but the voice has a hollow, metallic ring to it. A woman practicing this facade often overdoes her makeup. Her frequent gestures are exaggerated. Her voice is a little louder than is pleasant. She is desperately trying to appear happy, as though she is not hurt, as though nothing is wrong inside, as though her life is perfect. What she is really thinking inside is: "I've been hurt so badly that I'm never going to give another person the opportunity to hurt me like that again. I will not let anyone come close enough to hurt me."

This type of reaction is often the response to betrayal, as I mentioned earlier. There are uncounted thousands of such people in American society today.

The third type of person becomes a fighter—one who fights everything. The order in which his reactions to rejection develop is usually like this: first, resentment; second, hatred; and finally, rebellion. Rebellion and witchcraft are twins, according to Scripture.

[23] *For rebellion is as the sin of witch-craft.* (1 Samuel 15:23 NKJV)

The sin of witchcraft means participating in the occult, which is the search for false spiritual experiences. The occult includes such things as Ouija boards, horoscopes, fortune tellers, seances, drugs—that whole realm. This sin is really the expression of rebellion. It is turning from the true God to a false god. It is the breaking of the first commandment, *"You shall have no other gods before me"* (Exodus 20:3).

Basically, the generation of young people growing up in the 1960s went the way of resentment, hatred, rebellion, and very often the occult. As I mentioned earlier, it was not because they were denied material things. Rather, it was because they did not feel loved, which was the one thing they really wanted.

Next, we will find out what Jesus has done to heal the wounds of rejection.

5

The Ultimate Rejection

The Ultimate
Rejection

Everything that God provides in the Gospel is based on fact. This can be summed up in three progressive *f*s—facts, faith, and feelings.

The Gospel is based on three simple facts: Christ died for our sins according to the Scriptures, He was buried, and He rose again on the third day. First Corinthians 15:3–4 indicates these facts are the basis of the whole Gospel. They are the *facts*.

Faith appropriates these facts. Faith begins with the facts; it accepts, believes, and acts on them. Then, after facts and faith, are feelings.

It makes all the difference in your life whether your faith is based on facts or on feelings. If it is based on feelings, you will be a very inconsistent, unstable person. Your feelings may change as circumstances change, but the facts will never change. If we are to make progress as Christians, we have to learn to believe the facts, even when our feelings cause us to doubt them.

To receive God's provision for rejection, there are two basic facts you must lay hold of. First of all, God did not make a lot of different provisions for each of the various needs of humanity. Instead, He made one all-inclusive provision that covers all the needs of all people: the sacrificial death of Jesus on the cross.

Secondly, what took place on the cross was an exchange that God Himself had planned. All the evil consequences of our sins came upon Jesus so that, in return, all the benefits of Jesus' sinless obedience might be made available to us. For our part, we have done nothing to deserve this, and we have no merits or rights by which we can claim it. It proceeded solely out of the unfathomable love of God.

Therefore, it is futile to approach God on the basis of some merit or virtue that we may imagine we possess. Nothing we have to offer of ourselves can be compared with the merit of the sacrifice that Jesus offered on our behalf. In contrast to the pure, holy Son of God dying in payment for our sins, *"all our righteous acts are like filthy rags"* (Isaiah 64:6).

This wonderful revelation has been summed up in a simple couplet:

How sovereign, wonderful, and free
  The love of God for sinful me!

As you read the following verses, you will discover various aspects of the exchange that took place on the cross.

[13] *Christ redeemed us from the curse of the law by becoming a curse for us, for it is written: "Cursed is everyone who is hung on a tree."*
[14] *He redeemed us in order that the blessing given to Abraham might come to the Gentiles.* (Galatians 3:13–14)

> [21] *God made him who had no sin to be sin for us, so that in him we might become the righteousness of God.*
>
> (2 Corinthians 5:21)

> [9] *For you know the grace of our Lord Jesus Christ, that though he was rich, yet for your sakes he became poor, so that you through his poverty might become rich.* (2 Corinthians 8:9)

> [9] *He [Jesus] suffered death, so that by the grace of God he might taste death for everyone.* (Hebrews 2:9)

Do you see the exchange? Christ took our curse so that we might have His blessing. He took our sin in order that we might have His righteousness. He took our poverty so that we might have His wealth. He took our death in order that we might have His life. Isn't that beautiful?

This exchange also has implications for us concerning shame and rejection. The writer of Hebrews said:

> [2] *Let us fix our eyes on Jesus, the author and perfecter of our faith, who for the joy set before him endured the cross, scorning its **shame**.*
>
> (Hebrews 12:2, emphasis added)

Jesus was well aware of the shame and public humiliation that He would experience on the cross. In fact, one of the primary objectives of crucifixion was to shame the person. As the person hung naked on the cross, spectators walked by, made derogatory remarks, and sometimes even did obscene things, which I will not describe.

In a prophetic vision Isaiah glimpsed the sufferings of Jesus seven centuries before they actually took place:

> [6] *I offered my back to those who beat me, my cheeks to those who pulled out my beard; I did not hide my face from mocking and spitting.* (Isaiah 50:6)

Jesus willingly endured mocking for us on the cross. What does God offer us in return? Again, we turn to Isaiah:

> [7] *Instead of their shame my people will receive a double portion, and instead of disgrace they will rejoice in their inheritance.* (Isaiah 61:7)

Holy Spirit joy

In place of the word *disgrace,* I would say *embarrassment* or *humiliation.* Instead of personal shame, embarrassment, and humiliation, God offers us honor and joy. Hebrews 2:10 further tells us that through the suffering and death of Jesus, God purposed to bring *"many sons to glory."*

Joy, honor, glory—all are offered to us in the place of shame and humiliation. Now we come to the deepest wound of all—rejection. Jesus endured a double rejection: first by men and then by God Himself.

Isaiah clearly portrayed the rejection of Jesus by His fellow countrymen:

> [3] *He was despised and **rejected** by men, a man of sorrows, and familiar with suffering. Like one from whom men hide their faces he was despised, and we esteemed him not.*
> (Isaiah 53:3, emphasis added)

Still worse things were to happen to our Savior. The last moments of Jesus on the cross are described in Matthew:

> [45] *From the sixth hour* [midday] *until the ninth hour* [three o'clock in the afternoon] *darkness came over all the land.*
> [46] *About the ninth hour Jesus cried out in a loud voice,* "Eloi, Eloi, lama

sabachthani?"—*which means, "My God, my God, why have you forsaken me?"*

[handwritten: He felt separation from God the Father!]

[47] *When some of those standing there heard this, they said, "He's calling Elijah."*

[48] *Immediately one of them ran and got a sponge. He filled it with wine vinegar, put it on a stick, and offered it to Jesus to drink.*

[49] *The rest said, "Now leave him alone. Let's see if Elijah comes to save him."*

[50] *And when Jesus had cried out again in a loud voice, he gave up his spirit.*

[handwritten: the ultimate sacrifice for humans to be reconciled]

[51] *At that moment the curtain of the temple was torn in two from top to bottom.* (Matthew 27:45–51)

For the first time in the history of the universe, the Son of God prayed, but the Father did not answer Him. God averted His eyes from His Son. God stopped His ears at His cry. Why? Because at that time Jesus was identified with our sin. The attitude of God the Father toward Jesus had to be the attitude of God's holiness toward our sin—the refusal of fellowship, a complete and absolute rejection. Jesus did not endure that for His own sake, but instead to make His soul a sin offering for us.

It means a lot to me that Jesus spoke in Aramaic at that agonizing moment on the cross. I have witnessed this behavior when visiting people in the hospital. When people are under real pressure, desperately sick, maybe at death's door, they often revert to the language they first learned in childhood. I have observed this many times, but I remember it so vividly with my first wife, Lydia. As she breathed her last, she whispered, *"Tak for blodet; tak for blodet,"* which means "Thank You for the blood" in Danish, her mother tongue.

This passage gives such a clear picture of the humanity of Jesus: as He suffered intense pain and agony, His mind went back to the language He had spoken in His childhood home. He cried out in Aramaic.

Think of that awful darkness. Think of the loneliness, the sense of being absolutely abandoned—first by man, then by God. You and I may have experienced some measure of rejection, but never has it been in that measure. Jesus drained the cup of rejection to its bitter dregs. He should have been able to live several hours longer on the cross, but He died of a broken heart. What broke His heart? The ultimate rejection. ✗

And then, look at the consequence, which was so dramatic, so immediate:

> ⁵¹ *At that moment the curtain of the temple was torn in two from top to bottom.* (Matthew 27:51)

no more separation

What does that mean? Simply that the barrier between God and man had been removed. The way was opened for man to come to God without shame, without guilt, without fear. Jesus took our rejection so that we might experience His acceptance. That is the meaning of the torn curtain. The rejection of His Father was more than Jesus could bear. But, thank God, the result for us is direct access to God.

Look now at how God has worked out and completed our acceptance:

> ³ *Praise be to the God and Father of our Lord Jesus Christ, who has blessed us in the heavenly realms with every spiritual blessing in Christ.*
> ⁴ *For he chose us in him before the creation of the world to be holy and*

blameless in his sight. In love
⁵ *he predestined us to be adopted as his sons through Jesus Christ, in accordance with his pleasure and will—*
⁶ *to the praise of his glorious grace, which he has freely given us in the One he loves.* (Ephesians 1:3–6)

no greater love than this!

What was God's eternal purpose, even before creation? That we might become His children, His sons and daughters. That could only be achieved through the substitutionary death of Jesus on the cross. When Jesus bore our sins and suffered our rejection, He opened the way for our acceptance. For just that time, Christ lost His status as God's Son in order that we might gain status as God's sons and daughters.

The New King James Version offers a special insight in this passage: *"To the praise of the glory of His grace, by which He has made us accepted in the Beloved"* (v. 6). That is the remedy for rejection—the realization that Jesus bore your rejection so that you might have His acceptance.

Ponder the depth of that revelation! We are the objects of God's particular loving care and attention. We are number one on His list of things to take care of in the universe.

He does not push us away into a corner and say, "Wait over there. I'm busy. I don't have time for you now."

And never does some angel say, "Don't make a noise. Daddy is sleeping."

God says, "Come in. You are welcome. I am interested in you. I love and want you. I've been waiting a long time for you."

In the parable of the prodigal son in Luke 15:11–32, God's heart toward us is represented by the father, who longed for his son to return so much that he was out watching. No one had to come and tell him, "Your son is coming home." The first one to know it was the father. God's attitude toward us in Christ is like that father's. We are not rejects; we are not second-class citizens; we are not slaves.

When the prodigal came back, he was willing to be a servant. He intended to say, *"Father,...make me one of your hired men"* (Luke 15:18, 19). But, as the prodigal confessed his sins, his father cut his words off and never allowed him to say, "Make me one of your hired servants."

On the contrary, the father said, "Bring out the best robe. Put shoes on his feet, a ring on his finger. Kill the fatted calf! We're going to have a good time. *'For this son of mine was dead and is alive again; he was lost and is found'*" (v. 24).

The whole household was turned upside down to welcome the prodigal as he returned. It is like that in heaven. Jesus said, *"There will be more rejoicing in heaven over one sinner who repents than over ninety-nine righteous persons who do not need to repent"* (Luke 15:7). That is how God welcomes us in Christ.

Here, then, are the two facts you need to lay hold of. First of all, Christ bore our rejection on the cross, along with all of the shame and betrayal, agony and heartache. In fact, He died of a broken heart.

Secondly, we are accepted because of His rejection. We are accepted in the Beloved. It was an exchange. Jesus bore the evil that we might receive the good. He carried our sorrows so we might have His joy.

Sometimes all you need is to grasp these two facts. Several years ago at a big camp meeting, as I was on my way to a preaching assignment, I literally bumped into a lady who was going rapidly in the opposite direction. Breathlessly, she said, "Oh, Brother Prince, I was praying that if God wanted me to speak to you, we would meet."

"Well," I said, "we've met! What's the problem? I can give you about two minutes because I'm due to preach." She started to talk, but after about half a minute, I interrupted her. "Wait, I know what your problem is. I don't need to hear any more," I said. "Your problem is rejection. I've got the answer. Listen. I want you to pray these words out loud after me."

I did not tell her in advance what I was going to say. I simply prayed extemporaneously, and she followed me phrase by phrase.

Father God,
I thank You that You love me; that You gave Jesus, Your Son, to die on my behalf; that He bore my sin; that He took my rejection; that He paid my penalty. Because I come to You through Him, I am not rejected; I am not unwanted; I am not excluded. You really love me. I am really Your

child. You are really my Father. I belong in Your family. I belong to the best family in the universe. Heaven is my home. I really belong. Oh, God, thank You, thank You.

After we finished, I said, "Amen, good-bye, I have to go," and took off.

About a month later, I got a letter from the lady. After describing the encounter, she said, "I want to tell you, those two minutes you spent with me and the prayer that I prayed have completely changed the whole of my life. I've been a different person ever since."

As I read her letter, I understood what had happened to her at the moment of praying: she had passed from rejection to acceptance.

God's family is the best family. There is no family quite equal to the family of God. Even if your own family did not care for you, your own father rejected you, your mother never had time for you, or your husband never showed you love, bear in mind that God wants you. You are accepted; you are highly favored; you are the object of His special care and affection.

Everything He does in the universe revolves around you.

Paul said to the Corinthians—who were not exactly top-class Christians—"*All this is for your benefit*" (2 Corinthians 4:15). Everything God does, He does for us. You will not get conceited when you realize that—instead, it will humble you. There is no room left for conceit when you see the grace of God.

It is most significant that, before His crucifixion, Jesus' last prayer with His disciples was for those who followed Him then as well as for those who would follow afterward. (See John 17:20.) That prayer concerned our relationship with God as our Father and ended this way:

> ²⁵ *Righteous Father, though the world does not know you, I know you, and they know that you have sent me.*
> ²⁶ *I have made you known to them…*
> (John 17:25–26a)

How did Jesus make God known to us? As Father. The Jews had known God as Yahweh for fourteen centuries, but the only Person who could introduce Him as

Father was His Son. Six times in this prayer for His disciples, Jesus addressed God as Father (vv. 1, 5, 11, 21, 24, 25).

When Jesus prayed, *"...and [I] will continue to make you known..."* (v. 26b), He was saying that He would continue to reveal God as Father. Then we come to the purpose of this revelation:

> [26] *...in order that the love you have for me may be in them and that I myself may be in them.*   (John 17:26c)

I understand this to mean that because Jesus is in us, God has exactly the same love for us as He has for Jesus. We are as dear to God as Jesus Himself is. However, there is also another aspect to this. Because Jesus is in us, we can love God in the same way that Jesus loves Him.

This represents the ultimate purpose of the earthly ministry of Jesus: to bring us into the same love relationship that exists between the Father and the Son. This has two aspects: not only does the Father have the same love for us that He has for Jesus, but also we can reciprocate with the same love for the Father that Jesus has.

The Beloved Apostle told us, *"There is no fear in love. But perfect love drives out fear"* (1 John 4:18). As we develop this love relationship with God, it leaves no room for guilt, for insecurity, or for rejection.

Perhaps you have unhappy memories of a human father. God intended every father to demonstrate what He Himself is, but many fathers have failed. Yet, you still have a heavenly Father who loves you, who understands you, who thinks the best of you, and who plans the best for you. He will never abandon you, never misunderstand you, never take sides against you, nor will He ever reject you.

For some, the simple declaration of acceptance in Christ and the fatherhood of God resolves the problem of rejection. But for others, that may not be enough to solve the issue. If you feel that your situation is not yet resolved, you may need further help. Follow on with me in the next chapter as I explain certain practical steps you can take to make God's provision effective in your life.

6

How to Apply the Remedy

How to Apply the Remedy

By this point, you have allowed the Holy Spirit to insert His probe into your wound, and He has exposed the foreign body that was causing the pain and the infection. Are you now ready to accept God's remedy? If so, there are five successive steps you need to follow.

Step 1. Recognize the nature of your problem and call it by its right name—rejection. God always has to bring us to the moment of truth, even though it may seem devastating and extremely painful, before we can receive His help.

Step 2. Take Jesus as your pattern.

²¹ Because Christ suffered for you, leaving you an example, that you should follow in his steps. (1 Peter 2:21)

How did Jesus meet rejection? For three and a half years, He had completely given His life to doing good, to forgiving sin, to delivering demon-oppressed people, to healing sickness. At the end of that period, the Roman ruler offered a choice to Jesus' own people, the Jews. He was willing to release from prison either Jesus of Nazareth or a criminal named Barabbas, who was guilty of political insurrection and murder.

By one of the most amazing and tragic decisions in all of human history, the people rejected Jesus and chose Barabbas. So, the mob cried out, "Away with Jesus! Crucify Him! We don't want Him. We'll have Barabbas, the rebel and the murderer."

In response, Jesus prayed for those who had crucified Him:

³⁴ Father, forgive them, for they do not know what they are doing. (Luke 23:34)

The second step, therefore, is to forgive. This is not an easy thing to do. In fact, left to yourself, you are incapable of doing so. However, you are not left to yourself. As you come to this moment, the Holy Spirit is right there with you. If you will yield to Him, He will give you the supernatural grace you need.

You may say, "But the person who hurt me is dead, so why do I need to forgive him?" Whether he is dead or alive is not important. It is for your sake that you are forgiving, not for the other person.

I know a fine, young, Christian man who heard this message. He realized that for years he had carried bitterness, resentment, anger, and rebellion against his father, who was dead. He took his wife on a journey of several hundred miles to the cemetery where his father was buried. Leaving his wife in the car, he went alone to his father's grave. He knelt there and for the next several hours emptied out all his poisonous attitudes. He did not get up until he knew he had forgiven his father. When he walked out of that cemetery, he was a different person. His wife testifies today that she has a brand-new husband.

His father had died, but his resentment had remained very much alive.

There is something especially important about parent-child relationships. Young people in particular need to remember this.

The only one of the Ten Commandments with a promise directly attached to it is this:

> [16] *Honor your father and your mother, as the LORD your God has commanded you, so that you may live long and that it may go well with you.*
> (Deuteronomy 5:16)

You can be sure of this: if you do not honor your parents, your life will never go well; but if you do, God will favor you with a long, blessed life. (See Ephesians 6:2–3.)

You may say to me, "My mother was a prostitute; my father was an alcoholic. Do you expect me to honor them?" Yes, I do—not as a prostitute and not as an alcoholic, but as your mother and father. It is God's requirement.

When I was newly saved and baptized in the Holy Spirit, I thought I knew so much more than my parents. Mark Twain once quipped that when he came back home after he had been away for a number of years, he was surprised at how much his parents had learned in the meantime! Well, I was like that, but one day God showed me this principle: if you want it to go well with you, you have to learn to honor your parents. My parents have both passed away now, but I thank God that I really learned to show them honor. I think that is one reason why it goes well with me.

I have seen both sides of this principle. I have seen the people who honored their parents and were blessed, and I have seen the people who refused to do it, and their lives never really went well for them. Their lives were never totally blessed of God.

The failure to forgive is one of the most common barriers to God's blessing. This principle also applies to the relationship between husbands and wives. I remember talking to a lady who had come to me for prayer and deliverance. I said to her, "You are going to have to forgive your husband."

She said, "After he ruined fifteen years of my life and ran off with another woman?"

I said, "Well, do you want him to ruin the rest of your life? If so, just keep on resenting him, because that will do it."

Remember, it is not the one who is resented that suffers the most. It is the one who resents. As somebody said about the man with the ulcer: "It's not what the man is eating; it's what's eating the man."

Forgiveness is not an emotion; it is a decision. Do not say, "I can't." In actuality, you are saying, "I won't." If you can say, "I won't," you can also say, "I will." Your fleshly nature may not be able to forgive, but you can choose to forgive by asking God to work His forgiveness in and through you. When the Holy Spirit enables you (and He will), you *can* forgive—if you *will*.

Step 3. Make a conscious decision to get rid of the bad fruit that rejection has produced in your life, such as bitterness, resentment, hatred, and rebellion. Remember that young man in the cemetery! These things are poison. If you nourish them in your heart, they will poison your whole life. They will cause you deep emotional problems and quite likely physical problems also. Say with a decision of your will: "I lay down bitterness, resentment, hatred, and rebellion."

Counselors say to cured alcoholics, "Resentment is a luxury you can no longer afford." That is true for all of us. No one can afford resentment. It is too expensive.

Step 4. In this step you simply need to receive and believe what God has already done for you.

> *highly favored*
>
> [6] [God] *has made us **accepted in the Beloved***.
> (Ephesians 1:6 NKJV, emphasis added)

When you come to God through Jesus, you discover that you are already accepted. God has no second-class children. He does not just tolerate you. He loves you. He is interested in you. He cares for you. Look at these beautiful words in Ephesians:

> [4] [God] *chose us in [Christ] before the foundation of the world, that we should be holy and without blame before Him in love,*
> [5] *having predestined us to adoption as sons by Jesus Christ to Himself, according to the good pleasure of His will,*
> [6] *to the praise of the glory of His*

grace, by which He has made us ac-cepted in the Beloved.

(Ephesians 1:4–6 NKJV)

[handwritten: highly favored]

God's purpose from eternity was to make us His children, which He accomplished through the death of Jesus for us on the cross. The only thing you need to do is to believe that God wants you to be His child. When you come to God through Jesus, He has already accepted you.

Step 5. Accept yourself. Sometimes this is the hardest step of all. I tell Christians, "Never belittle yourself. Never criticize yourself. You did not make yourself. God made you."

Ephesians 2:10 tells us, *"We are God's workmanship."* The Greek word translated here as "workmanship" is *poiema,* from which we derive the English word *poem.* It suggests an artistic achievement. We are God's masterpieces. Of all God created, He has devoted the most time and care to us.

[handwritten: artistic achievement]

Amazingly enough, He went to the scrap heap for His material! You may be looking back over a record of failures and false starts—over a broken marriage, over children who went wrong, over financial disaster. You may label yourself a failure, but God calls you, "My son, My daughter." You can accept yourself because God has accepted you. When you come to God in Jesus, you become a new creation.

> [17] *Therefore, if anyone is in Christ, he is a new creation; old things have passed away; behold, all things have become new.*
> [18] *Now all* [this is] *of God, who has reconciled us to Himself through Jesus Christ.* (2 Corinthians 5:17–18 NKJV)

You can no longer evaluate yourself on the basis of the way you lived before you came to Christ, because you have become a new creation since then. Now, your only true standard of self-evaluation is what God says about who you have become in Jesus. As you repeatedly declare who you are in Christ according to God's Word, you will begin to override the old, negative self-talk and learn to accept yourself.

Have you followed through those five steps? If so, it is time now for you to claim your release and to pray a prayer that will set the seal on what you have learned about God's acceptance of you.

You can pray simply in your own words. But if you are not quite sure what to say, here is a pattern prayer that you may make your own:

Lord Jesus Christ,
I believe that You are the Son of God and the only way to God. You died on the cross for my sins, and You rose again from the dead. I repent of all my sins, and I forgive every other person as I would have God forgive me. I forgive all those who have rejected me and hurt me and failed to show me love, Lord, and I trust You to forgive me.

I believe, Lord, that You do accept me. Right now, because of what You did for me on the cross, I am accepted. I am highly favored. I am the object of Your special care. You really love me. You want me. Your Father is my Father. Heaven is my home. I am a member of the family of God, the best family in the universe. I am accepted. Thank You! Thank You!

One more thing, Lord. I accept myself the way You made me. I am Your workmanship, and I thank You for what You have done. I believe that You have begun a good work in me and You will carry it on to completion until my life ends.

rejection
self-pity

And now, Lord, I proclaim my release from any dark, evil spirit that took advantage of the wounds in my life. I release my spirit to rejoice in You. In Your precious name, Amen.

This is the moment to be released from any evil spirit that may have been tormenting you. If you feel some force struggling against the prayer you have just prayed, that is an evil spirit. Quite possibly a word may form in your mind—rejection, resentment, self-pity, hatred, death, or other similar names. That is the Holy Spirit revealing the identity of your enemy. Renounce it by name, and then release it. No matter what way it manifests itself, you must expel it. Breathe it out, sob it out, or scream it out—but get it out!

This is the moment you have been longing for. Don't worry about your dignity right now! Accept all the help the Holy Spirit gives you.

As you experience release, begin to praise God out loud: "Lord, I thank You. Lord, I praise You. Lord, I love You! Thank You for liberation. Thank You for setting me free. Thank You for all You have done for me."

Thanking God sets the seal on your release. Now you are ready for your new life of freedom.

7

Acceptance
in God's
Family

Acceptance
in God's Family

One more important step remains in achieving complete acceptance: finding acceptance by God's people. This means discovering your place in the body of Christ. As Christians we are never isolated individuals. We are brought into a relationship with our fellow believers. That relationship is one of the ways in which our acceptance is worked out in our day-to-day living. Acceptance by our Father in heaven is the first step and the most important. However, acceptance also has to find expression in our relationships with our fellow believers. Christians collectively constitute one body, with each Christian a member of that body. As Paul wrote:

> [4] *Just as each of us has one body with many members, and these members do not all have the same function,*
> [5] *so in Christ we who are many form one body, and each member belongs to all the others.* (Romans 12:4–5)

Since we are members of one body, and each of us belongs to all the others, we can never find full satisfaction, peace, or acceptance apart from the other members.

> [14] *Now the body is not made up of one part but of many.*
> [15] *If the foot should say, "Because I am not a hand, I do not belong to the body," it would not for that reason cease to be part of the body.*
> [16] *And if the ear should say, "Because I am not an eye, I do not belong to the body," it would not for that reason cease to be part of the body.*
> (1 Corinthians 12:14–16)

You are a part of the body. You may be a foot, a hand, an ear, or an eye. However, you are incomplete without the rest of the body, and the rest of the body is incomplete without you. That is why it is so important to find your place in the body.

> [21] *The eye cannot say to the hand, "I don't need you!" And the head cannot say to the feet, "I don't need you!"*
> [22] *On the contrary, those parts of the body that seem to be weaker are indispensable,*
> [23] *and the parts that we think are less honorable we treat with special honor.*
>   (1 Corinthians 12:21–23)

Thus, none of us can say to our fellow believers, "I don't need you." We all need one another. God created the body so that the members are interdependent. None of them can function effectively alone. That applies to each one of us. That applies to you. You need the other members, and they need you. Finding your place in the body will make your acceptance a real, day-to-day experience.

Another picture the New Testament gives of Christians is that of a single family unit. We are all members of one and the same family. The great prayer that Jesus

taught His disciples begins with those two
significant words, "Our Father." That tells
us two things. First, we have a Father who
is God. That means we are accepted verti-
cally by God. But, the first word is *our* and
not *my,* which tells us that we are members
of a family, with a lot of other children in
that family. Our acceptance becomes effective horizontally only when we find and fit
into our place in the family. Thus, we find
vertical acceptance with God and horizon-
tal acceptance in God's family. ╈

> [19] *Consequently, you are no longer for-*
> *eigners and aliens, but fellow citizens*
> *with God's people and members of*
> *God's household* [or members of
> God's family].   (Ephesians 2:19)

The alternative is to be foreigners and
aliens. We do not like those words, *foreigners* and *aliens.* I immigrated to the United
States in 1963, and I did not become a citi-
zen until 1970. For seven years I was an
alien in this country. Most people who become citizens at birth have no idea what it
is like to be an alien.

Every January I had to fill out a form
for the Department of Justice, notifying

them of where I was residing. They had to be able to find me if they had questions about me—or if they wanted to deport me. I also could not vote in federal or local elections.

If I went out of the country, on my return I had to join a special line, separate from U.S. citizens, to have my passport checked. Then, along with my passport, I had to present a little green card, stating that I was a resident alien.

There are distinctions and differences between citizens and foreigners. You do not really belong as long as you are an alien. However, God says, "You are no longer an alien. You do belong. You are inside. You are part of My family." Yet, that only becomes real to you when you find your place in the family. The psalmist wrote:

> [6] *God sets the lonely in families....*
> (Psalm 68:6a)

Are you lonely? Millions of people are. They have not realized that God provides families for the lonely.

> [6] *...He leads forth the prisoners with*

*singing; but the rebellious live in a
sun-scorched land.*   (Psalm 68:6*b*)

God's purpose is to bring you into a
family. In doing so, He breaks the chains
that bind you, and He brings you into happiness. Only people who refuse God's lead-
ership have to dwell in a scorched land.

You may wonder just how you should
become a part of God's family. You can join
groups with many different names—
church, fellowship, mission, and so on. The
name is not important. But it is not always
easy to find the kind of group that will
make you truly accepted. In my book *The
Marriage Covenant,* I have listed nine
questions that anybody seeking such a
group should ask before he or she joins:

1. Do they honor and uplift the Lord Jesus Christ?
2. Do they respect the authority of
   Scripture?
3. Do they make room for the moving of
   the Holy Spirit?
4. Do they exhibit a warm and friendly
   attitude?
5. Do they seek to work out their faith
   in practical, day-to-day living?

6. Do they build interpersonal relationships among themselves that go beyond merely attending services?

7. Do they provide pastoral care that
embraces all your legitimate needs?

8. Are they open to fellowship with
other Christian groups?

9. Do you feel at ease and at home
among them?

If the answer to all or most of these
questions is affirmative, you are getting
warm. Continue to seek God, however, until you receive definite direction from Him.
Keep in mind that you probably will not
find the perfect group.

Now you know the way to escape from
your loneliness and your sense of being on
the outside looking in. Become part of a
living organism, a living body. Find your
place and your function, and you will experience fulfillment.

At the end of *The Marriage Covenant*,
I suggest a prayer to be prayed by anyone
longing to find his or her place among
God's people. I am including it here. If it
expresses how you feel, read it through,
and then put it in your own words. That
way you can make it your prayer.

Heavenly Father,

I have been lonely and unful-filled, and I acknowledge it. I long to *"dwell in your house"* (Psalm 84:4), to be part of a spiritual family of committed believers. If there are any barriers in me, I ask You to remove them. Guide me to a group where this longing of mine can be fulfilled, and help me to make the needed commit-ment to them. In Jesus' name, Amen.

If you have sincerely prayed that prayer, I promise you that something is going to happen in your life. God is going to move. He will give you new direction and new associations. He will open new doors for you. He will bring you out of that parched land and cause you to be a mem-ber of His family and a part of His body.

8

The Flow
of Divine
Love

The Flow of
Divine Love

In briefly reviewing the information we have covered, we have learned that many people suffer from the spiritual wounds of rejection, betrayal, and shame. Specific causes include parental neglect, divorce, public humiliation, and child abuse.

Jesus provided healing for our wounded spirits through a series of exchanges on the cross. He was rejected by God and man in order that we might be accepted by God and God's family. He suffered shame so that we might share in His glory. He died our death in order that we might receive His life.

Recognizing what Christ has done may bring release to some; others may need to take further steps. These are:

1. Let the Holy Spirit help you identify how or where you have been wounded by rejection.
2. Forgive the people who have harmed you.
3. Lay down the destructive fruits of rejection such as resentment, bitterness, hatred, and rebellion.
4. Accept that God has accepted you in Christ.
5. Accept yourself.

The primary result of rejection is the inability to receive love from others and to communicate love to them. That is why rejection is one of the greatest hindrances to divine love. God works in our lives to bring us to the knowledge of divine love.

Here I am not referring to the love that God shows toward us but to the way in which God's love first flows into us and then out through us to the world at large.

In this process there are two successive phases: first, God's love is *outpoured;* then God's love is *outworked.* The first phase is a tremendous supernatural experience; the second is the gradual, progressive formation of godly character.

It is illuminating to contrast this kind of love with mere human love. In my youth I especially admired the writings of William Shakespeare. Shakespeare was preoccupied with two human experiences, love and death. He hoped that love would somehow provide an escape from death.

There appeared in his sonnets someone who came to be known as "the dark lady." She was apparently the object of Shakespeare's passionate affection but did not fully requite it. In one sonnet he tried to convince her that though she might grow old, his love through his poetry would make her immortal.

Shall I compare thee to a summer's day?
Thou art more lovely and more temperate:
Rough winds do shake the darling buds of May,
And summer's lease hath all too short a date:
Sometime too hot the eye of heaven shines
And often is his gold complexion dimmed;

And every fair from fair sometimes declines,
By chance or nature's changing course
   untrimmed;
But thy eternal summer shall not fade,
Nor lose possession of that fair thou ow'st;
Nor shall death brag thou wander'st in his shade,
When in eternal lines to time thou grow'st:
   So long as men can breathe or eyes can see,
   So long lives this, and this gives life to thee.[1]

That was the best his love could offer her—the immortality of his poetry. Sure enough, it has lived on for four hundred years, but the lady died.

Shakespeare had a very high expectation of love, and I would say he was probably disappointed. Having gone that way myself, I think I understand his disappointment.

For twenty-five years I searched for something permanent and satisfying in poetry, philosophy, and the world, with all its pleasures and intellectual challenges. The more I looked, the less satisfied I became. I had no idea what I was looking for. However, when the Lord revealed Himself to

---

[1] Stanley Wells, ed., *Shakespeare's Sonnets* (Oxford: Oxford University Press, 1985), 32.

me and baptized me in the Holy Spirit, I knew instantly that this was what I had been seeking all the time. I had attended church services for twenty years, but no one had ever told me about it. God poured into my heart an overwhelming love that finally, completely satisfied me.

Now we will explore what happens when we love people with God's version of love—not Shakespeare's, but God's. In Romans we read this tremendous statement:

> [5] *And hope does not disappoint us, because God has poured out his love into our hearts by the Holy Spirit, whom he has given us.* (Romans 5:5)

Hope, or love, is never disappointed when it is fixed in God because the love of God has been poured out into our hearts— the totality of God's love. God withholds nothing. He just turns the bucket upside down and pours out the whole thing when He gives us the Holy Spirit.

During World War II, when I served in the British army as a medical orderly or attendant, I was overseas for four and a half years, mainly in North Africa, and then in what was at that time Palestine. I spent one year in the Sudan, which is a bleak, dry, desert land. To the natural human mind, no perception of the Sudan or of the Sudanese people is very attractive. However, I had been baptized in the Holy Spirit, and God had shown me that He had a destiny for me there. He began to give me a supernatural love for the Sudanese.

The army stationed me for a short while at a railway junction in the northern Sudan called Atbara. I was in charge of a small reception station for military patients. I think it had three beds. I worked in liaison with a civilian doctor in the city, but I was my own boss for the first time in my military career. For the first time, too, I had a bed to sleep in. Additionally, among the issued equipment in this reception station were long, white nightgowns. At that time I had spent about three years sleeping in my underwear, and I was tired of it. So, I availed myself of the facilities, put on a flannel nightgown, and slept in a bed.

One night as I lay in bed, the Spirit of God came upon me while I was in intercessory prayer for the people of the Sudan.

The prayer had nothing to do with my natural feelings toward them at all, but I could not sleep. I was driven by an inner urgency, which I know was the prompting of the Holy Spirit. I found myself praying with a supernatural love far above the level of anything I could achieve by my own reason or emotion.

Sometime in the middle of the night, I got out of bed and began to pace the floor. Suddenly, I was aware that my white nightgown was actually shining. I realized that for those brief moments I had become identified with our great heavenly Intercessor, the Lord Jesus.

Later, the army transferred me to a small hospital in a miserable place in the Red Sea hills, where the local tribal people were called Hadundawa. They were a wild, fierce people who knew no religion but Islam. About one hundred years previously, they had fought a brief war against the British. At that time, the British soldiers had nicknamed the Hadundawa "fuzzy-wuzzies" because the men fixed their woolly hair with mutton fat in a bushy style that stood out about eight inches from their scalps.

All my fellow soldiers were discontented, but I spent eight of the happiest months of my life there because God had given me His love for those people. As a result, I had the privilege of winning to the Lord the first member of the Hadundawa tribe who had ever professed faith in Christ. When I left, it broke my heart to say good-bye to that man and that place.

In the Sudan at that time, I experienced some small measure of the outpoured love of God for those people. Later, however, I came to understand that this needed to be made complete by God's love developed in my character.

About a year later in Palestine, when I met my first wife, Lydia, and saw the girls she was caring for, the Lord again filled my heart with His wonderful love. At that time neither Lydia nor I had any thoughts of marriage, but eventually we were married. God had once again poured out His supernatural love in my heart, but it still did not make me the kind of person I ought to have been. I was often selfish, irritable, impatient, self-centered, and insensitive, none of which exemplified Christ's character or image.

I came to understand that a supernatural experience of the outpoured love of God is wonderful, but much more needs to be done to form our characters. God has to take us beyond the supernatural outpouring of love to the formation of a character that consistently expresses His love. That is a process, a long process, and it requires God's patience to take us through it.

In this process of character formation, the wonderful Word of God plays a vital part.

> [4] *The man who says, "I know him," but does not do what he commands is a liar, and the truth is not in him.*
> [5] *But if anyone obeys his word, God's love is truly made complete in him. This is how we know we are in him:*
> [6] *Whoever claims to live in him must walk as Jesus did.* (1 John 2:4–6)

Notice how this verse mentions the Word of God, not the Spirit of God. We are not talking about a supernatural experience but about the slow, steady formation of character that develops through consistently obeying the Word of God. If we faithfully follow Christ's guidance by walking as He did in obedience to the Scriptures, God's love will gradually be brought to completion or maturity in us.

That verse is like the two faces of a coin. On the one side, the proof of our love for God is that we obey His Word. It is in vain to claim that we love God when we do not obey His Word. On the other, as we obey His Word, God works out His love in our characters. These two aspects cannot be separated because they make up a whole.

The process of character building has seven successive phases, according to the apostle Peter:

> ⁵ *But also for this very reason, giving all diligence, add to your faith virtue, to virtue knowledge,*
> ⁶ *to knowledge self-control, to self-control perseverance, to perseverance godliness,*
> ⁷ *to godliness brotherly kindness, and to brotherly kindness love.*
>
> (2 Peter 1:5–7 NKJV)

We start with the foundation. *"Giving all diligence, add to your faith virtue."* The starting point with everything God does is faith. There is no other place to begin. But after God has given us faith, there has to be a process to character development.

Let us follow these seven successive steps of character building as we find them in 2 Peter 1:5–7.

"Add to your faith virtue." For the word *virtue,* I like the alternate translation of "excellence." Excellence is the mark of a Christian. Never be sloppy in anything you do. If you were a janitor before you were saved, be a better janitor afterward. If you were a teacher before, be a better teacher after. If you were a nurse, be a better nurse. We must add excellence to our faith.

For five years I was principal of a teacher training college in Kenya. My primary purpose was to win my students to Christ. When they professed Christ and were baptized in the Holy Spirit, they would sometimes say to me, "You can go easy on me now," or "You are going to expect less of me because I am a Christian."

I would reply, "On the contrary, I expect much more of you now. If you could be a teacher without Christ and the baptism, you ought to be twice as good a teacher when you have Christ and the baptism. I am going to expect more, not less."

God honored my commitment to excellence. The third year I was in charge of that college, the graduating class consisted of fifty-seven well-trained men and women. In the final examinations, every student passed in every subject. A representative of the education department of the Kenyan government who was responsible for teacher training colleges came. He congratulated me personally and said, "In all our records we have never had results like these."

It was because I followed the Scriptures' demand for excellence. Our examination results impressed the secular authorities more than any doctrinal statement we might have issued. Christianity is no excuse for being sloppy. In fact, the sloppy Christian is denying his faith.

"To [excellence] *knowledge."* Primarily, this means the knowledge of God's will and the knowledge of His Word. Secular knowledge is often important to acquire, especially in developing the necessary skills for your vocation, but even more important is learning what God's will is for your life

in every circumstance, which can be discovered by thoroughly studying His Word.

"To knowledge [add] *self-control."* There is a point beyond which you cannot go in character development if you do not learn to control yourself, your emotions, your words, your appetites, and all· the things that motivate you.

"To self-control [add] *perseverance."* Stick it out! Again, there is a point beyond which you will never advance if you do not learn to persevere. Otherwise, every time you are about to attain the next stage of development, you will give up.

"To perseverance [add] *godliness."* Godliness, or holiness, is developed by allowing the Holy Spirit to control your temperament and every aspect of your being.

"To godliness [add] *brotherly kindness* [or love]."* This becomes our corporate testimony to the world. Jesus said, *"By this all will know that you are My disciples, if you have love for one another"* (John 13:35 NKJV).

"To brotherly kindness [add] *love"*—divine, agape love. This is the consummate,

ideal, perfect kind of love that God has for us. It begins when the Holy Spirit pours out God's love in our hearts. However, it comes to its culmination in the development of our characters. The difference between brotherly love and divine love is that in brotherly love we love our fellow Christians who love us; in divine love we love those who hate us, persecute us, and are altogether unloving and unlovable.

This brings us right back to the same issue of rejection. What is the evidence that you are healed of this wound? Can God give you divine love for the person who has rejected you? Can you go back to an unloving parent and say, "I love you"? Can you say a prayer for your former spouse and ask for God's blessing on him or her? It is the most unnatural thing in the world, but then God's love is supernatural—far above anything that proceeds out of our own efforts.

This is perhaps the greatest of all the blessings that follow from the healing of the wounds of rejection, betrayal, and shame. You can become a vessel of God's love to others who have been wounded just as you were.

About the Author

D erek Prince was born in India in 1915 of British parents. He was educated as a scholar of Greek and Latin at two of Great Britain's most famous educational institutions—Eton College and Cambridge University. From 1940 to 1949, he held a Fellowship (equivalent to a resident professorship) in Ancient and Modern Philosophy at King's College, Cambridge. He also studied Hebrew and Aramaic at Cambridge University and at the Hebrew University in Jerusalem. In addition, he speaks a number of modern languages.

In the early years of World War II, while serving as a hospital attendant with the British Royal Army Medical Corps, Derek Prince experienced a life-changing encounter with Jesus Christ, concerning which he writes:

> Out of this encounter, I formed two conclusions that I have never since had reason to change: first, Jesus Christ is alive; second, the Bible is a true, relevant, up-to-date book. These two conclusions radically and permanently altered the whole course of my life.

At the end of World War II, he remained where the British Army had placed him—in Jerusalem. In marrying his first wife, Lydia, he became a father to the eight adopted girls in Lydia's Jerusalem Children's Home. Together the family saw the rebirth of the State of Israel in 1948. While serving as educators in Kenya, Derek and Lydia Prince adopted their ninth child, an African baby girl.

After Lydia died in 1975, Derek Prince married his second wife, Ruth, in 1978. He had met Ruth, like his first wife, while she was serving the Lord in Jerusalem. Ruth's three children bring Derek Prince's family to a total of twelve, with many grandchildren and great-grandchildren.

Derek Prince's nondenominational, nonsectarian approach has opened doors for his teaching ministry to people from many different racial and religious backgrounds. He is internationally recognized as one of the leading Bible expositors of our time. His daily radio broadcast, *Today with Derek Prince,* reaches more than half the globe, as it is translated into Arabic, five Chinese languages (Mandarin, Amoy, Cantonese, Shanghaiese, Swatow), Mongolian, Spanish, Russian, and Tongan. He has published more than thirty books, some of which have been translated into more than fifty foreign languages.

Through the Global Outreach Leaders Program of Derek Prince Ministries, his books, audio cassettes, and videotapes are sent free of charge to hundreds of national Christian leaders in the Third World, Eastern Europe, and Russia.

Now past the age of seventy-five, Derek Prince still travels the world—imparting God's revealed truth, praying for the sick and afflicted, and sharing his prophetic insight into world events in the light of Scripture.

The international base of Derek Prince Ministries is located in Charlotte, North Carolina, with branch offices in Australia, Canada, Germany, Holland, New Zealand, South Africa, and the United Kingdom.